Folktales
of the
Yeats Country

EILY KILGANNON

Illustrated by
CATHY HENDERSON

THE MERCIER PRESS
CORK and DUBLIN

The Mercier Press Limited
4 Bridge Street, Cork
24 Lower Abbey Street, Dublin 1

British Library Cataloguing in Publication Data
Kilgannon, Eily
    Folktales of the Yeats Country
        1. Irish tales – Anthologies
        I. Kilgannon, Eily
        398.2'1'09415

    ISBN 0-85342-861-1

> *Have not all races*
> *Had their first unity*
> *From a mythology that*
> *Marries them to rock*
> *And Hill?*
> *W. B. YEATS*

Printed by Litho Press Co., Midleton, Co. Cork.

Contents

Acknowledgments

I wish to express my sincere thanks to Seán Feehan who encouraged me to write *Folktales of the Yeats Country*. My very special thanks go to Oonagh Dennis for typing the manuscript. My thanks go too to Liz Parsons and John C. Ryan who proof-read the tales. My personal thanks go to my nephew Barry Sweeny whose budding artistic talent opened my mind to new angles on the stories.

A very special word of thanks to John McGloin and to Stephen Connelly for the story of the Dabharchú.

I am most grateful to the Head of the Department of Irish Folklore at U.C.D. for permission to use material from their Folklore library, and the Sligo County library for access to their local history files.

I also acknowledge permission of A. P. Watt Ltd on behalf of Michael B. Yeats and Macmillan, London, Ltd, for permission to quote extracts from the works of W. B. Yeats.

1

Children of
the Mermaid

A mermaid found a swimming lad,
Picked him for her own,
Pressed her body to his body,
Laughed; and plunging down
Forgot in cruel happiness
That even lovers drown.

W. B. Yeats

In the old days, the chieftains and rulers of Tireragh were the O'Dowds. Tireragh lies to the west and south of the bay of Sligo, and O'Dowd's country covered all the beautiful sea shores of Enniscrone, Easky and Aughris. At the time of our story, the O'Dowd chief was looking around to find himself a wife. While surveying his lands along the sea-shore, he saw the most beautiful girl he had ever seen perched on a rock, combing her long golden hair.

She sat all alone. She was unaware that anyone was watching her. As he stared at the beautiful girl he noticed the bottom half of her body – she was a mermaid. O'Dowd knew all the old stories of the mermaids and he came out to Cruchancormia to see her every morning. Each day he fell more and more in love with the mermaid.

'If only,' he thought, 'if only I could find her magic mantle.'

Now all in Tireragh know that once the mermaid loses her magic mantle, she loses her 'fish-body' at the same time, and while she still longs for the sea, her nature becomes human, like ours.

On the seventh morning, when O'Dowd looked from the cliff, he was distressed because he could not see his mermaid. But then, he looked again – what was that amongst the rocks? Quickly he came down to the rocky shore and sure enough, there among the rocks was his beautiful mermaid, asleep, and enveloped in her beautiful magic mantle.

Very quietly, and as slowly and gently as he could, O'Dowd slipped off her mantle. Almost not allowing himself to breathe, he moved back towards the rocks and hid the cloak.

Then the mermaid began to stir. Her fishy tail began to disappear, and on the rock, as O'Dowd emerged, sat a beautiful girl. O'Dowd advanced, approached the maiden and wooed her. She told him that her name was Nemain. She did not tell him, if she remembered, of the sea-nymph's body from which she had emerged. Happily, Nemain fell in love with O'Dowd, and he carried her away from the sea-shore to be his bride.

O'Dowd and Nemain were happy together. He was careful to ensure the magic mantle was always carefully hidden. He knew that should she see it, the pull of the ocean and her old life among the sea-creatures would be too great to hold her.

The years rolled by happily. Seven children were born to O'Dowd and Nemain and, as the children of the chieftain, their lives were indeed good and they were happy.

One day, however, when the youngest boy, Phelim, was four years old, O'Dowd decided to move the magic mantle to a more secure hiding-place. He had constantly changed the secret nooks in which it was hidden. Phelim watched his father as he carried the cloak. He could not take his eyes off the mantle. How it flashed, glistened and always seemed to change colour and shade! He was filled with delight, and ran to describe it to his mother. Phelim was surprised that she did not share his joy at its beauty. She did not laugh in her usual way. She only asked, with a cold stare in her eye, where his father had left the mantle before he went out.

The little boy could now only stare at his mother. She seemed overcome. She raced to the hiding place. As she saw her beloved mantle she was filled with a longing for the free life of the ocean. She was torn apart when her eyes met with Phelim's questioning look.

But the call of the sea ran through her body like a pulse. She looked out of the door of the O'Dowd Castle at the Atlantic breakers as they billowed in the wind and broke on the rocky sea-shore. She quickly summoned her seven children, and together they set out for the sea-shore. As she moved from the last blade of green grass to the edge of the shore, she looked back quickly at the land. The children were happy to visit the shore with her, as previously they had always gone with their father.

Nemain put her hand inside the magic mantle and drew out the magic wand. She touched each child, one after another, with the wand. The instant the wand touched the children's heads they were turned into stone. Seven stones stood on the shore where before there were none.

Nemain regained her mermaid body, plunged in to the ocean, and was never again seen in Tireragh.

2

Omra and Romra

Dance there upon the shore;
What need have you to care
For wind or water's roar?

W. B. Yeats

Overlooking the beautiful lake named Lough Gill which drains into Sligo Bay is a hill known as Cairn's Hill. Beneath a mound on this high hill, two chieftains were buried thousands and thousands of years ago. Some say that the chieftains were brothers, and one was named Omra and the other Romra. They ruled over Sligo, but not the town that we know today. The city over which they had command is now buried deep in the waters of Lough Gill.

Romra had a beautiful daughter whose name was Gile. Romra kept his family away from the visits and eyes of his fellow-chieftains, but at last one day he introduced Omra to Gile. Gile was truly beautiful and Omra fell in love with her. Her manner was kind and charming. Gile too was attracted to Omra.

Very soon, they began to meet secretly. For a long time they kept their love a secret from Romra. But

11

one day, as they walked by the sea shore admiring the majestic Ben Bulben on one side and Knocknarea on the other, Romra spotted them. He was filled with anger and fury. He did not stop to think, but dashed forward in a fit of temper to attack Omra. He wished to kill him and there in front of Gile, her lover Omra fell dead by her feet, killed by the hand of her own father.

Omra had fought back and Romra was badly wounded. He lived only a few more days, and then died of the wounds.

The beautiful young Gile was distraught. She could not contain her grief – her father and lover had been so prematurely and savagely removed from her life. Her grief knew no bounds and so she killed herself. Gile's nurse-maid had left off comforting her just a short while before. The nurse-maid began to shed her tears of grief for Gile and it is said that so great was the grief and so plentiful were her tears that they filled the valley and that is how the lake Lough Gile or Lough Gill was made and was named.

3
Finn Mac Cumhail
and the Bald Man

Finn Mac Cumhail and his mighty army were out hunting one day on their favourite hunting mountain – Ben Bulben. The mountain was always lucky for Finn – especially for hunting hawk and deer. But this was a strange day and they captured nothing.

They were discouraged as usually their hunting provided them with a good supper. In the evening Conan the Bald and Finn sat down with the rest of the Fianna and began to play at dice. They played, and at one point Finn hesitated. A voice behind his shoulder told him how to play. Finn looked back and saw a Bald Man standing behind him. He did not know him, but followed the advice in any case and won.

'That was good, Bald Man,' said Finn.

'It was not good,' said the Bald Man, 'because my wife has gone off with another man.'

'That is bad, Bald Man,' said Finn.

'That is not bad,' said the Bald Man, 'because I have my children.'

'That is good, Bald Man,' said Finn.

'That is not good,' said the Bald Man, 'because I

have only one acre of land, and that has to support all of us.'

'That is bad, Bald Man,' said Finn.

'That is not bad,' said the Bald Man, 'because I have sixty stacks of oats on that acre.'

'That is good, Bald Man,' said Finn.

'That is not good,' replied the Bald Man, 'because when they are ready, a great flood comes and sweeps away the stacks of oats.'

'That is bad, Bald Man,' said Finn.

'That is not bad,' replied the Bald Man, 'because on the river I have a windmill, and it harvests every single grain for me.'

'That is good, Bald Man,' said Finn.

'That is good,' replied the Bald Man.

Finn was astounded that the Bald Man agreed with him for once, but he did not show surprise.

'It is good,' he continued, 'because as well as feeding my children with this harvest, I feed twenty litters of pigs, and one of the litters is just nicely fat to make us all a fine supper. I am inviting you and your men to come with me to feast on these fine pigs.'

'And where do you live may we ask?' enquired Finn.

'There are four ends to the world and whichever you choose, you shall arrive at my door,' said the Bald Man.

The Fianna set off and after a lot of walking and argumentation they arrived at a wood. There they saw a light which they followed. This light led them to a house, and who should emerge to greet them but the Bald Man?

'By now you must be starving,' said the Bald Man.

The Fianna were very hungry indeed. 'Wait,' the Bald Man said, 'The pig litters are all sleeping now. In with them is the old sow. You must kill the litter without waking any pig and without waking the old sow.'

The Fianna with all their skill at arms and in combat considered that this would be a very easy task. Conan began the kill for the Fianna and he was followed by nine others. The Bald Man had given them a large hammer.

However, none succeeded in killing the pigs until the Bald Man did so himself. The pigs were prepared for the table and boiled.

'There is no doubt Finn but this will be a scrumptuous meal for you and your hungry followers,' said Conan.

'That is good,' said the Bald Man, 'if you can keep it away from those coming in the door now.'

Quickly, as reflected their training, the Fianna lifted their eyes from table to door. But, when they cast their eyes back to the feast again, everything had disappeared! Once again, they were seated on the grass at the foot of Ben Bulben playing dice!

The Fianna were sorely disappointed. Their hunger felt more intense now. And so ended a mysterious day for the Fianna.

About a week later when the Fianna were in the same area, the Bald Man cropped up again. This time he addressed Finn differently!

'It is true Finn, I played a trick on you the last day. I didn't mean any harm by it. Today, I do invite you all to dine with me, and this time you won't have to kill the pigs yourselves!'

This time nothing disappeared, and Finn, Conan and the Fianna and the Bald Man had a royal feast on his pigs!

4

At the Hawk's Well

In Sligo's district on Mount Gam's high side
A fountain lies not washed by ocean's tide,
Each circling day it different water brings –
The fresh, the salt, from its alternate springs.
The Wonders of Ireland – O'Flaherty's Ogygia

The Hawk's Well lies on the slopes of the Ox Mountains, or Sliabh Gamh, and thousands of years ago, this Hawk's Well had been listed in the *Mirabilia Hibernia* or *The Wonders of Ireland*. Although the well is far from the Atlantic Ocean, it ebbs and flows with the tide. Its water is salty for part of the day, and for the rest of the day it holds sweet fresh water. The Hawk's Well can cure, but its water can never be boiled.

The oldest story of the Hawk's Well is that Gamh, a servant of the ruler Eremon, was beheaded. Gamh's head was thrown into the well and so the tide rushed underground to wash away the servant's blood with fresh and salt water.

For many years, Gamh's story may have been lost or forgotten, but the Hawk's Well at Tullaghan

19

became famous again when St Patrick preached in Ireland.

The Saint was on top of the peak in County Mayo, on the mountain now known as Croagh Patrick. From the top of the mountain, he banished the serpents and the demons into the sea, and out of Ireland. But one demon escaped.

The escapee demon was called Caorthannach, also known as the Fire-Spitter. It is even said that Caorthannach was the devil's mother. St Patrick saw the Fire-Spitter slide down the side of the mountain, and he was determined to pursue her so that not even one demon would remain on the island of Ireland. At the foot of the mountain, St Patrick was given a good horse to pursue the Caorthannach. She spat fire all around as she fled northwards.

The Fire-Spitter knew that Patrick would need water to quench his thirst as he rode in hot pursuit. So, she poisoned all the wells as she ran from the Saint. The Caorthannach was right. St Patrick became more and more thirsty as he pursued the demon. At last, in County Sligo, on the slopes of Sliabh Gamh, at Tullaghan, he was overcome by the thirst and he prayed for a drink. As he prayed, suddenly his horse stumbled. He fell from the animal's back, and his hand hit off a stone, and then his back hit off the stone. On the spot where he landed, a well sprang up beside him. This was the Hawk's Well. The well was small, with a circular stone at its base. The water was brackish, but St Patrick was glad to taste its sweet freshness. He drank and drank of the Hawk's Well, and soon felt refreshed and ready to take up the chase after Caorthannach, the Fire-Spitter.

He lay in wait in a hollow beside Carraig-an-Seabhach, the Hawk's Rock. The Caorthannach had taken a different route from St Patrick, still polluting all the wells as she sped along. St Patrick lay in wait for the Fire-Spitter as she approached the Hawk's Well. Out he sprang and with one word he banished the Caorthannach, the last demon-serpent in Ireland, until she drowned in the Atlantic Ocean. Behind him the tide flowed into the Hawk's Well. To this day, the marks of St Patrick's hand and back, where he fell from the horse, and the mark of his horse's hoof can be seen on the stones by the well.

Two enchanted trout inhabit the well to this very day. It is said that at various times, people without respect for the sacredness of the well have taken the trout and broiled and eaten them. Although this has happened more than once, the two trout always re-appear in the well – and there they can be seen as lively as ever.

Word of St Patrick's revival at the Hawk's Well, and of the banishment of the Fire-Spitter spread quickly. The well at Tullaghan in the Ox Mountains became a place of prayer, cures and pilgrimage and celebration for many, many years. For centuries it was the location of the biggest pattern in the area. It took place every year on Garland Sunday – the last Sunday in July. Patterns were the lively festivals which continued right up to the first half of this century.

The pattern at the Hawk's Well in honour of St Patrick was always a great occasion. Tents were erected, dealers came to trade their wares, pipers, fiddlers and musicians arrived. Poteen-makers came too, in great numbers, and the festivities sometimes got out of hand as the poteen flowed. During the reign of Queen Anne, an Act was passed imposing fines and whippings on persons attending pilgrimages at holy wells.

But Garland Sunday was a pattern which everybody enjoyed, and so instead of cancelling the midsummer celebration, the festivities were moved from Tullaghan Hill at the Hawk's Well to Trá Eochaile, or Ballisodare Bay, and so the festivities were merely transferred. The clergy had warned the people against the pattern, because of the excesses of previous years.

In 1826 the biggest crowd ever gathered on the strand to celebrate the pattern of St Patrick at the Hawk's Well. The clergy had forbidden the people to attend. The sun shone warmly on the gathering and the happy throng, including fiddlers and poteen-makers thought that God was on their side, as the weather was so beautiful. Celebrations were in full swing when all of a sudden, a fierce storm burst through the sun. Thunder rolled, lightning flashed and the rain poured from the heavens. The small tents could not shelter the huge crowds of people, all exposed to the angry elements on the sea shore. The tornado continued all through the night. It was called the 'night of the big thunder' for generations afterwards. Only at daybreak did the storm abate.

That night in 1826 dampened the spirits of the people for the Garland Sunday pattern. They felt that the wrath of God had come upon them. And so the pattern was never revived after that awesome day. The tradition of over 2,000 years was broken by the storm. Neither fines, nor whippings nor warnings from the altar had succeeded in breaking that tradition going back into the mists of time, but the mighty elements did just that.

The Hawk's Well is still one of the wonders of Ireland. Now, very few people witness the flow and ebb of its tide. From this tide sprang the forgotten story of Gamh – whose head was cast on its water. Later the story of Patrick and Caorthannach sprang from its waters. Now this too is forgotten.

Maybe the stones of the Hawk's Well have still not told the whole story, and maybe the stones may yet give up the secret of this mysterious place.

5

St Patrick Visits Coney Island

Oisín:
   'O Patrick! for a hundred years
   At evening on the glimmering sands,
   Beside the piled-up hunting spears,
   These now outworn and withered hands
   Wrestled among the island bands.
   O Patrick! for a hundred years
   We went a-fishing in long boats
   With bending sterns and bending bows,
   And carven figures on their prows
   Of bitterns and fish-eating stoats.'

St Patrick:
      'Be still: the skies
   Are choked with thunder, lightning,
      and fierce wind,
   For God has heard, and speaks His angry mind;
   Go cast your body on the stones and pray,
   For He has wrought midnight and dawn and
      day.'

                                 W. B. Yeats

24

In the bay of Sligo there is an island which in olden times was called Inis Coinín – the island of the rabbits. The name of Coney Island is well known now because an area, including a beach near New York, is called after our Coney Island.

But long before Columbus discovered America, St Patrick discovered Ireland. He travelled the length and breadth of the country telling the people about Christ and Christianity and baptising the Irish race so that most of them became members of the church of Christ.

Everywhere he went he found old customs and old rituals which were followed by everybody he met with diligence. And so instead of outlawing the old ways, St Patrick gave them a new Christian meaning. He was welcomed as a guest wherever he went. ·

The old Celtic rules for honouring and welcoming a guest were very strict, and usually guests were treated royally. St Patrick arrived on Coney Island, and was welcomed on the shore. He preached the gospel of Christ and baptised the island people. He hoped that one day it would be possible to build a church there.

He was invited to eat with one of the island families. The lady of the house – her name was Stoner – was in quite a fuss as she did not have any rabbit available to cook. However, strangely enough, all sat down to eat what looked like a delicious rabbit stew.

St Patrick blessed the food and the hands that made the food. He lifted his knife to begin to eat when suddenly a dog appeared at the door of the house, and with that there was a stir on his plate! Whoops!

26

a cat jumped up from his plate and bounded out the front door.

The lady of the house had a very red face and St Patrick glared around and jumped to his feet in great anger and said: 'The people of this island must never forget what happened to St Patrick when he visited you. Never, therefore, shall a church be built on the island.' Seeing the dismay on the faces of the islanders as he strode out into the sun, and casting his eye across the bay, he added one thing: 'One thing I will guarantee to the people of Coney Island is that on every Sunday of the year forever it will be possible to cross the seas to go to church on the mainland. Neither tide nor storm can ever prevent you from travelling to do homage to God on any Sunday.'

And so it has been. No church was ever built on the island. Islanders can either cross the seas by boat to Rosses Point, or cross the strand when the tide is low to Strandhill. Whatever the storm it has always been possible for the Coney Islanders to reach a church on a Sunday, without getting their feet wet, and this is St Patrick's legacy to them.

6

Foster-Brothers, Blood-Brothers

(i) FISH, MAN, HORSE AND HOUND

Long, long ago in Ireland in the County of Sligo, there lived a King with his Queen. He was a powerful ruler and she was beautiful, but alas they had no children! The King's chief adviser Fergus, it was said, was one of the Sidhe, the Faery People. The King asked Fergus for his advice as he was anxious to have children to inherit the kingdom.

Fergus gave his advice:

Send a servant to the shores of Lough Gill, the bright lake, where it touches Dooney Rock, and bid him fish. Bid him takë home the seventh fish he catches, to be prepared for the Queen's breakfast by the royal cook. The cook must roast the fish by the fire, making sure that neither blob or blister appears on the skin.

Everything was arranged as Fergus ordered. But while the fish was heating a little blob appeared. The cook took a quick glance around to check that nobody was looking, put her finger to the skin to smooth it down, and then put the finger to her mouth to cool it – and so she tasted the fish!

The fish was served up to the Queen for breakfast. She ate it with relish. What remained was thrown out

in the yard where the mare and the greyhound ate the left-overs.

And before the year was out, to the great delight of all the kingdom, the Queen had a young son! The cook also had a young son, the mare had two foals and the greyhound had two pups!

(ii) THE WELL OF BLOOD AND HONEY

It was the custom in the olden days in Ireland that children were sent off to foster-parents who cared for them until they were grown up. And so it was with the Queen's son, Dara and the cook's son, Conn.

When they were eighteen summers old they returned to County Sligo. But almost immediately the Queen became very vexed. This was because both Dara and Conn were so alike that nobody could tell which was which!

The Queen went to Fergus, the chief adviser. She did not want the cook's son to enjoy the same privilege as the King's son. Fergus solved the problem for the Queen. He ordered one of the servants to put a mark on the neck of Dara, the Queen's son. He gave the signal, and told the servant that as they walked through the palace door Dara, the royal one, would bow his head, but Conn, the cook's son would only laugh.

The mark was made, and soon afterwards the Queen asked Conn, the cook's son to leave the palace. The boys had thought that they were real brothers and the Queen's words hurt them both deeply. Conn left immediately. Dara tried to stop him. He followed him to the well at the edge of the wood which surrounded their home. The boys were broken-hearted at the parting but Conn made a solemn promise to Dara:

> If harm ever comes to me Dara, the water on the top of this well will turn to blood, and the water below will turn to honey.

Dara gave Conn one of the pups and one of the horses for his journey, and he was carried along by the sidhe-gaoth, which is the Faery Wind.

(iii) THE THREE GIANTS

The sidhe-gaoth carried Conn to a King's house in a far distant place. Conn asked if the King wanted a servant. The King needed a herdsman for his cows. Conn's job was to drive the four and twenty cows to pasture in the morning, and to return them to the byres for milking in the evening.

Conn soon saw that there was no pasture for the cows, but only a field full of stones. Conn scouted around the area in search of a grassy field and soon found one but it was surrounded by a high wall. Conn demolished an area of the wall and drove in the King's cows to the sweet grass. He climbed an apple-tree in the field and surveyed the happy cows chewing the cud as he feasted on the apples. He began to congratulate himself on his good discovery when the owner of the field made an appearance. The owner was a giant.

'Fee-faw-foh-fum, I smell the blood of a Sligoman,' grunted the giant. Conn tried to hide in the tree, but the giant roared: 'Come down from the apple-tree you little dwarf. I see you well. I gauge that you are too big for one mouthful, but too small for two mouthfuls. Come down and I'll grind you up to make snuff for my nose.'

Conn shook at the sight of the giant, but said bravely: 'As you are strong, be merciful.'

The giant was not listening. This time he bellowed: 'Come down, I tell you, you dwarf or I'll tear you and the tree asunder.'

So Conn came down. He looked very tiny beside

the giant. 'Choose,' said the giant, 'choose dwarf –
will we fight with red-hot knives, or will we fight
hand to hand standing on red-hot flags?'

'I'm more used to red-hot flags at home,' said Conn
as he gathered all his courage, 'and your dirty feet
might sink while mine will rise.'

'Red-hot,' said the giant.

And so the fight between Conn and the giant
began. It was a long fight and a hard fight. The birds,
small animals and insects of the field were terrified to
move, and the battle lasted the whole day long. At
last, at evening, a little bird perched on Conn's shoulder and whispered to him: 'If you don't finish the
giant off by sunset then he will finish you off.' So
Conn mustered all his strength so that he brought the
giant to his knees.

The giant begged for mercy: 'Give me my life,' he
croaked, 'and I'll give you the best gift I have.'

'What's that?' Conn asked very quickly.

'It is a sword,' said the giant, 'a sword that nothing
can stand against.'

Conn eyed the giant's prized sword.

'Try it out,' said the giant, 'on that ugly black
stump of a tree.'

'I see nothing uglier or blacker than your own
head,' said Conn, and with one whistle through the
air, the sword cut off the giant's head. The giant's
head flew through the air; Conn cut it in two as it
descended, and with that, the head spoke in a
threatening tone: 'It is well for you that I did not join
the body again.'

Conn replied saying, 'You had no chance', but his

34

heart pounded within him when he thought of what could have happened if the head had rejoined the body!

Conn had no friends at the palace so he told nobody of his adventure with the giant when he returned with the cows. Everyone at the palace was amazed to find that the cows had so much milk that evening. At the King's table, his daughter the princess whose name was Alanna said to her father: 'Father, each evening I have always heard three fearsome roars from outside the gates of the palace, and tonight I have heard only two.' The King paid little attention to this, but he was very pleased that the cows had milked so well.

And so the next day, Conn drove out the cows, spied a second field of grass surrounded by a wall, and everything happened exactly as it had the day before, but this time the giant who appeared had two heads and he spoke to Conn from both mouths. The fight was long and hard again, and the friendly bird gave Conn the warning once again when it was time to muster his strength. But this time, the best gift which the two-headed giant offered was 'a cloak that when worn makes the wearer invisible.' Conn took the cloak, donned it, and as before drew the sword on the two-headed giant. The sword whistled through the air, the two heads flew high in the air, and Conn made four heads of the two. Once again, the heads spoke to Conn from all four mouths and said: 'It is well for you that we did not join the body again.' Conn shivered at the thought!

That night the cows gave so much milk that vessels

could not be found to contain it all.

Conn kept all his secrets to himself and set out in search of fresh pastures and fresh adventure the next day. Once again, a new field was found as before and this time the giant had four heads. All happened as on the previous two days and Conn with a masterly stroke converted the four heads into eight heads as the giant's sword whistled through the air. This time the giant's gift was a pair of shoes which when worn meant the wearer could travel faster than the wind.

So now, Conn possessed the giant's sword, the 'Invisible' cloak, and the 'Faster Than Wind' shoes. But he kept his secret and that night when the King whose name was Labhras summoned him and asked: 'Conn, why is it that the cows are giving so much milk these days? Are you bringing them to other grass?'

'No,' Conn answered.

And then the King asked Conn a strange question: 'Conn, my daughter heard mighty roars outside the palace walls. People here used to say it was the roar of a giant, but since last night the roars have ceased. Have you seen the giant, Conn?'

'No,' he answered.

Somehow or other Conn felt he would have need of the giant's gifts very soon.

(iv) THE SERPENT AND THE BULLY

Conn's 'feeling' was right. King Labhras had a great problem of which Conn had not heard. That was because the problem occurred only once in every seven years. A great serpent demanded the life of one princess every seven years. King Labhras thought that he had made provision for the next visit of the serpent. He had kept a young man known as 'the Bully' underground for seven years and had been feeding him so that he could fight the serpent and his daughter Alanna would not become its next victim.

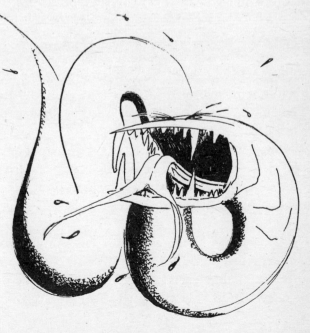

Alanna told Conn the story of the serpent, and told him how the next day she would be sent to the sea-shore where the Bully would fight the serpent, and save her life. Alanna confided in Conn that she had little faith in the Bully as only his body and not his spirit and courage had been prepared for the fight. 'Please help me Conn,' she implored.

'No Alanna,' Conn made a tight-lipped reply.

The next day Conn watched from afar as Alanna and the Bully set off for the sea-shore. The Bully had neither heart nor courage for the fight. And so he tied Princess Alanna to a tree so that the serpent could swallow her up without delay, and he climbed up an ivy tree where he would be well-hidden.

Conn watched as the Bully hid himself. He disguised himself so the Princess would not recognise Conn the cowherd, and he carried with him the giant's sword. He ran forward. The princess explained her predicament to the stranger (as she thought!) who said: 'If you would let me sleep for a while with my head in your lap, you could wake me when the serpent is coming.' The princess put her trust in the stranger.

She called Conn in terror as the serpent approached from the sea. He picked up the giant's sword and beat the serpent back to the sea. Then Conn released the Princess Alanna from the tree where she was tied and sped off.

The Bully emerged from his hiding place and returned to the palace with the Princess. He admitted to King Labhras that he had not fought the serpent as he was timid after being shut up underground for so long, but promised to fight the serpent the next day.

The next day, the Princess and the Bully made their way to the shore-line of the serpent again. The Bully did exactly what he had done the day before – he tied the Princess up and then disappeared in hiding.

This time, Conn donned the giant's cloak. Once again Alanna did not recognise him. Again, he slept with his head in her lap awaiting the serpent. The terror which the Princess felt as she saw the great threatening shape of the princess-eating serpent appear was more intense than the day before, because now she remembered how savagely and viciously he had fought. The serpent's nostrils bulged as he approached the tree to which she was tied, and Conn leaped to the rescue. Today the fight was longer and more vicious but sometimes Conn used the cloak's power to make himself invisible, and so he was able to surprise the serpent and at last drove him back to the sea.

The Princess was released by Conn. Again, he disappeared quickly. The Bully told the King that he had taken a friend to fight the serpent, but that on the next day he himself would tackle the princess-eating beast.

The third day came. The Princess made her way with the Bully to the sea-shore. She hoped that the stranger who had fought for her life twice already would come to the rescue again today. As before, he had made no promise, but she had her hopes. This time, she had made a preparation for his appearance, and carried with her a small, sharp blade, and a little sewing bag.

The Bully did his usual cowardly deed tying Princess Alanna to the tree. He scampered off to his usual hiding-place well covered by the ivy leaves.

In spite of her terror, Alanna was happy when she saw Conn appear. As on other days, she did not recognise him as her father's cowherd. Before going to sleep he vowed to the Princess that this time he would put an end to the serpent forever.

As soon as he fell asleep in her lap Princess Alanna took out her sharp blade and cut off a lock from his hair. She carefully bound it up and hid it in her sewing bag. She also took off one of his shoes and this too she hid in her sewing bag.

The vicious serpent frightened her for the third time. Conn leapt up at her call and with one thrust of the giant's sword he pierced the back of his neck. Blood and water splurged and spouted from the serpent's neck. It ran inland for fifty miles until it emptied itself into the river Shannon. The Princess was overjoyed but saddened as Conn disappeared with his usual speed.

Today the Bully rushed down from the ivy tree, raced back to the palace, claimed that he saved the Princess' life and had put an end to the princess-eating serpent forever.

People rushed from far and near to congratulate the Bully. A feast was made ready for the wedding of the Princess and the Bully. But the Princess Alanna told the King that she would marry none but the man whose hair would match the lock of hair and whose foot would fit the shoe.

(v) CONN, THE COWHERD

So, the shoe was first fitted on the Bully. We know that the hair did not match and not even his big toe could fit into the shoe.

King Labhras was so happy that his daughter was alive that he went along with her demand, and so a great Ball was held so that all the nobility of the countryside could try the shoe and could check if the lock of hair matched their own.

The Princess Alanna was beautiful. There was now no danger from a princess-eating serpent and so all the nobility from far and near flocked to the Ball. It was even said that some of them had pieces cut off their toes! But although all the nobility were present at the Ball the shoe did not fit a single one.

Alanna was disappointed but was determined that she would not marry until the shoe was matched. The King was in a quandary – after all everyone had tried the shoe already!

Labhras the King sought advice. His advisor counselled that another Ball must be held, this time for the poor as well as the rich. The great Ball was held. The servants had strict instructions to try the shoe on every right foot. They were becoming exhausted, the crowd had been so huge, and all so eager to try the shoe. The King was becoming impatient. 'Is everyone here?' he asked the servants.

'All except the boy who tends the cows. He sleeps in the byre,' the chief servant replied.

'Take Conn in also,' said the King.

Conn had heard the King's voice. His heart missed a beat as he had come to love Alanna throughout his adventures with the serpent. He tried the shoe – it fitted. Gasps of astonishment could be heard! The lock of hair was set beside his hair – it matched exactly. Some of the young men fainted! The Princess Alanna gave a cry of joy and ran into Conn's arms.

And so Conn and Alanna were married and great feasting for three days and three nights celebrated the wedding. And they lived together in great happiness and peace for a time. But Conn's adventures were not all over. One final great adventure awaited him.

(vi) TWO RIBS OF HAIR

Conn often hunted the deer in the forests which he had now come to know so well all around the palace of Labhras the King. But one morning a strange thing happened. A deer with bells ringing stopped under Conn's window. The ringing of the bells seemed to say to Conn, 'Here is the hunt. But where are the huntsmen and the hounds?'

It was as though Conn was being compelled to hunt. Conn took his horse and his hound and set off to hunt the deer. The deer avoided Conn throughout the day, the graceful animal was always out of reach, on the hill when he was in the hollow valley and below when he rode on the hill. Conn was amazed that this deer was so skilful in avoiding him and as if by stealth, night began to fall. Conn followed the deer who now took to the woods. The deer led him to an old mud cabin, where an old woman sat by the fire. She looked to Conn, as he dismounted, as if she might be two hundred years old. Conn was in awe of the old, old woman but asked, 'Lady, did you see a deer pass this way?'

'No,' she replied, 'but it's too late now for hunting. Better to stay here for the night. Hunting is best in the early morning.' Conn thought that this was good advice, but enquired what he might do with his horse and hound.

'Here are two ribs of hair,' said the old crone, 'tie them up with these.'

Conn complied with this strange request and

43

returned to the hovel, but the woman's face had changed: 'You killed my three giant sons,' she chanted, 'and I'm going to kill you now.' She put on her hands strange grotesque gloves, each heavy with stones and with long nails protruding from them. She began to attack Conn with these terrible weapon-gloves. As she attacked, Conn began to remember the fights with her three giant sons whose heads he had split in two and he seemed to recall that these fights were much easier than this battle with their 200 year old mother. He began to feel the need of some help and shouted to his hound: 'Help, hound, help.' But as he cried for help to his hound the 200 year old woman cried: 'Squeeze, hair,' and the rib of hair on the hound's neck squeezed him to death.

Conn began again, and this time he called for help to his horse. This time the woman issued the same command: 'Squeeze, hair.' And so the faithful horse was choked to death. And then Conn passed out. The old woman kicked his body outside her door.

(vii) THREE GREEN STONES

Conn's blood-brother Dara was walking past the well on the outskirts of the wood surrounding his palace that morning when he noticed a drop of blood at the top of the well, and underneath he saw the honey.

Conn's old promise flashed to his mind immediately. He jumped on his fastest horse and asked the old Sidhe-Adviser, Fergus, how he might find Conn.

Fergus, sensing the urgency of the mission, whispered in the horse's ear. At the sound of his voice, the horse's ears pricked up and his hooves began to dance. Dara felt the strange rumblings of the sidhe-gaoth which spirited him far away from County Sligo. Suddenly in front of him he saw a deer and heard the sound of bells ringing as though they came from the deer.

The deer led Dara to the old woman's house. At first, she got a shock, so striking was the resemblance between Dara and Conn. But just as with Conn, she invited him to stay for the night. Dara, however, threw the ribs of hair which she gave him for his horse and hound into the fire. When he returned from outside, she took a sharp glance at Dara and said: 'Your brother killed my three sons. I killed him and now I'll kill you.' She slipped the grotesque gloves on to her long-nailed fingers and wizened hands, but this time as Dara lost strength and called for help to his horse and hound and as the old crone cried, 'Squeeze, hair,' the hair replied, 'I can't because I'm in the fire.'

The giants' mother knew then that she would be beaten. The hound put his teeth in her. Dara brought her to her knees and she cried for mercy: 'Give me my life, and I'll tell you how you can get your brother back again – and his hound and his horse.'

'How?' asked Dara quickly.

She pointed to a rod over the fire. Only then did Dara realise that the giants' mother must have witch's powers.

'Take down that rod. Take it to the three green stones outside the door. Strike the three stones gently with that rod. The three green stones are your brother, his hound and his horse. At the first strike, they will come to life again.'

Dara obeyed the command of the old crone. And all happened as she said. Conn looked dazed as he became human again. The old crone repented and vowed never again to take vengeance. Conn was overjoyed to meet his brother Dara from whom he had been separated during all the years of his adventures.

They journeyed back together to the palace of King Labhras. A great feast was held to welcome Conn's brother, Dara. The feasting lasted for three days and a half.

After one month, Dara was married to Alanna's sister and, without danger from giant, serpent or witch they all lived happily ever after.

7

The Stolen Bride

*(Adapted from The Land of Heart's Desire
– W. B. Yeats)*

*Come away, O human child!
To the waters and the wild
With a faery, hand in hand,
For the world's more full of
Weeping than you can understand.*

W. B. Yeats

The faery people in Ireland are the people of the De Danann. They lived under the ground and near the surface of the ground. They are 'the Forgetful People' and their most earnest wish is that they must not be disturbed.

My grandmother, when throwing out hot water at the back door at night, would always warn the Little People so that they would not be scalded. She would always use the words, 'Huda, huda, uisce salach,' which means, 'Beware, dirty water coming.'

But some people are very vulnerable to the fairies – babies and newly married brides. And sometimes the fairies are very active – on May Eve and at Halloween.

One May Eve long ago in County Sligo in the Bruin's house Bridget was working hard in the kitchen and she was being watched by her new daughter-in-law, Mary. Mary was the bride of her son Seán and she dreamt of the ribbons which Seán would bring home to her from the fair.

Bridget's husband Maurteen was helping her with the fire and Father Hart, the local priest, called to visit the family. Mary took up the book she was reading and when the priest asked her about the book Mary told him, in a trance-like state, of the story of Princess Edain who went off on a May Eve to the land of Faery. Maurteen was afraid when he heard Mary's voice and he asked the priest to use his influence to stop her reading. He was especially anxious because it was May Eve.

He checked if Mary had hung out the whin bushes to prevent the fairies from coming into the house. But Mary told that no sooner had she hung the yellow gorse on the wall than a child ran up and caught it in her hand and fondled it.

Suddenly Mary gives a start as she sees a child, as though of the woodland, stretch towards her with an empty cup, indicating her thirst. Mary takes milk to the child.

Then a little old man asks for a light for his pipe and Mary carries a lighted coal to the door. She meets her husband Seán at the door, but Seán has seen neither the child nor the old man.

Old Bridget feels the power of the Faery people pushing towards the house and she is upset that Mary has given milk and fire on May Eve.

Mary has grown restless – she is weary of her father-in-law's wisdom, Bridget's bitterness, the priest's piety and even of Seán's drowsy love. But with a few kind words from Seán she begins to consider that she may be selfish.

And just then, a child humming a strange tune, comes in by the door. Her manner is so mild and courteous that Bridget welcomes her warmly. She asks for bread and wine and then asks for a space to be cleared so that she can dance. She gets ready for the dance and is about to begin when she sees the crucifix hanging on the wall.

The strange child bawls and screams until the crucifix has been hidden from her sight. It is then that she dances and twirls her fingertips in a trance-like state over all in the house. She sings, as she dances:

> The wind blows out of the gates of the day,
> The wind blows over the lonely of heart,
> And the lonely of heart is withered away.

Mary is enchanted by the dance. Seán tries to coax her away from the child but all in vain.

The Faery child has cast a spell on the household and now begins to lure the newly married bride to the 'woods, and the waters and pale lights.'

Mary hesitates as she sees her husband's loving face. But the pull of the Faery-world is magnetic. And so Mary went

> To the waters and the wild,
> With a faery, hand in hand,
> From a world more full of weeping than
> She could understand.

8
The Last Wolf
in Ireland

Nowadays, there are no wolves in Ireland. Yet, in the very old stories, wolves formed part of the old life. There is a stone today in the Royal Irish Academy in Dublin, and this was originally in Ardnaglass Castle in Skreen in County Sligo. The stone depicts a dog killing a wolf.

Long ago, when O'Dowds were the chieftains in that part of Sligo, a wolf was wreaking havoc among the sheep in the area. In those times, most people lived on the land and there was consternation as night after night more sheep were killed by the savage wolf. What made it harder to bear was the fact that most people thought that there were no longer any wolves in Ireland.

O'Dowd was incensed that although cleared out all around the country one wolf still lived on to destroy his sheep. He had an excellent wolf dog, and so he released him to follow the last mad wolf on Ireland's shores. At first, there was a terrible chase – the O'Dowds watched from the vantage point of Ardnaglass. The chase continued, but at last O'Dowd's wolf dog was ahead and began to corner the wolf who had tired. A savage fight between the two animals followed, and at last a great cheer rose when O'Dowd's dog won the battle and the last wolf in Ireland had been eliminated.

To this day, the townland where the final fight occurred is called Carrownamadoo, to commemorate the victory of the dog.

9

The Rent in
the Breeches

Over one hundred years ago in Ireland, life was hard
for most people. Many people still remembered the
Great Famine when whole families and whole villages
were wiped out by the potato blight. Families had
died of the fever, some had died on the coffin-ships
on the way to the New World, some made it all the
way to America, and some stayed to struggle towards
a better life at home.

Many who stayed at home were tenant-farmers.
They rented their land from the landlord and paid a
high rent. This was difficult to accumulate and each
year they struggled to feed the family and pay the
rent. And so it was in Kilglass by the sea in County
Sligo, thirty miles from the town of Sligo, seven small
farms had a landlord named Lestrange, and owing to
the expense of travelling thirty miles, the farmers took
it in turn to go to Sligo to pay the rent for all seven.

The harvest was over, the rent had been put
together penny by penny, and once again it was time
to pay the landlord.

This year it was Mike Patrick's turn to go to Sligo.
But he refused. The total sum of twenty-seven pounds

was pressed into his hand. And still he refused to take his turn at travelling to town to pay the rent for the seven.

When his neighbours asked him why he would not travel, he replied that he was too poor. They just laughed at that excuse. All of them were too poor! And so they pressed Mike for the real reason why he refused to co-operate. He was always a helpful neighbour and this made them even more surprised.

Eventually, the truth came out. Mike Patrick blurted out, 'I have no breeches for going to town.' (In those days they always called trousers, breeches). Most of the others thought it was a joke that Mike did not have breeches. Still, when they remembered that most of their breeches had been sent to them by relations in America, and as Mike did not have any friends in America, they began to appreciate his problem.

Mike's nearest neighbour was Tadhg William and he offered Mike the loan of a pair of his breeches to go to town. Mike was happy to borrow them, he promised to return them safely, and with the twenty-seven pounds in rent and two shillings for his expenses he set off on foot north-eastwards to Sligo.

He began his journey in the middle of the night, and walked right through the dawn, still when he arrived at the rent office it was closed. Mike Patrick was disappointed; and he was tired and exhausted after his long trek.

He sought out the lodging-house and so he told his tale to the people of that house. They gave him supper and a candle to light his way to bed. As soon as he got into the room, he checked the door, but there was neither bolt nor lock on it. This made Mike feel most uneasy. He was carrying a lot of money. But he climbed into bed and realised he needed a good sleep so that he could be in the rent office early the next day. He was very tired. As soon as his head touched the pillow he was asleep.

Next morning, the lady of the lodging house was a bit surprised that Mike did not appear for breakfast. She was busy and soon forgot about him. However, as the morning wore on, and as she cooked the dinner, she sent her husband upstairs to check on the lodger.

Her husband found Mike in the bed, wide-awake. 'I thought you were anxious to go to the rent office early,' said the man of the house. 'Did you sleep in?'

'I did not,' answered Mike. 'I have been awake since the chimes went six o'clock. I have heard every chime of the clock since then.'

'What's wrong?' asked the landlord.

'I have no breeches,' answered Mike sadly. 'The breeches I had have disappeared. I am lying here all morning wondering what I will do.'

The husband consulted the lady of the house. At first, they thought that Mike's story was a peculiar one, but then they had seen him the night before with his breeches on and now they had disappeared! The lady of the house found a pair of breeches left by a previous lodger. Mike was in a state of panic. Here he was amongst strangers and the borrowed breeches and the precious rent money had disappeared, or most likely had been stolen. He fitted on the breeches which were offered by the landlady. They were too long and too wide. However, he rolled up the bottoms and tied them up under the knees with straw ropes so that they should not be so ill-fitting.

Mike Patrick opened the door of the office where the rent was payable. He told his story. At first, they doubted him. They thought it was much too unlikely and that it was just an excuse to put off paying the rent. But Mike's manner was so agitated and his whole appearance, especially the strange breeches, made them realise that something was amiss. And so Mike Patrick was told to return with the full rent in one week.

With a heavy heart, Mike started off on the long road home. He could not imagine what his fellow tenants would say to him when he got there. In each house, it was the last penny which had made up the rent. There would be no way of raising the money. And what would Tadhg William say about the loss of the breeches as well?

Mike went straight home to his own house that night. He tiptoed past the houses where he saw lights burning. He thought it would be better to wait for morning to break the bad news.

Mike Patrick slept very little that night in spite of his fatigue. He rose in the morning and told the story of what happened to one of his neighbours. 'How can I raise more rent?' he bellowed at Mike. 'You know that I sold the pig.'

He got the same kind of reception at the second house: 'Raise more rent? I'm ruined. I'll be evicted. The landlord will turn me out of house and home.'

Mike knew this would happen to all of them. He was near tears as he headed for the house of Tadhg William. Strangely, he thought that Tadhg had a mischievous glint in his eye as he spotted him in the distance piling turf against the wall. His dog Shep came to greet Mike. Tadhg set his eye on Mike as he told the story of the rent in the breeches.

'We must pay it,' said Tadhg.

Mike was astonished that he seemed to make light of the disaster. 'With what money?' asked Mike.

'With this money,' answered Tadhg and placed the twenty-seven pounds once more into Mike's hand. He was dumbfounded. Tadhg quickly went into the house and walked out carrying the breeches which Mike had worn to town.

Tadhg's faithful dog Shep had followed Mike all the way to Sligo it seemed because the animal arrived home to Kilglass with the breeches in his mouth!

Life went on for the seven tenant farmers. Mike had some repairs done to the long breeches and Shep was the talk and the toast of the parish!

(From the story heard from Rev. W. Canon Healy, Parish Priest, Kilglass Parish and relayed by M. Clarke, National Teacher, Kilglass to Irish Folklore Commission.)

10
The Giant's Stone-Throwing Competition

One day before the Fianna returned from hunting hawk and deer, as they stood at a place near the top of the Ox Mountains, with gigantic boulders and stones surrounding them, Caoilte and his clan challenged Finn to a stone-throwing competition.

The test was that the stone should land in the sea – in today's measurements that would be about twelve miles. So Caoilte and his clan lifted a large stone and sure enough it landed in the sea – just at the mouth of the Easky river.

Finn paused and was about to lift a large rock when he spied a gigantic boulder not far away. Not another man of the Fianna would even attempt to lift this boulder. The leader of the Fianna knew that to attempt the competition with such a large boulder was risky, but Finn faced every challenge bravely and he usually won.

The eyes of all the Fianna including his son Oisín, Diarmuid, Oscar and all the clan of Caoilte were on Finn. He lifted the boulder with ease and balance. He poised himself to throw the stone, and in the twilight he could see the brightness of the sea in the far

distance.

He threw it, the boulder hurled through the air, and it landed a great distance away. All eyes peered in the half-light, first at the flying rock and then at each other. Finn did not like to lose whether the challenge was at chess, on the battlefield or as a test of skill. But it was clear that the boulder had not reached the sea-shore. The stone was dry where it lay in a field at Killeenduff.

Finn flew into an angry rage. The Fianna laughed – only after he had leapt from the mountain and with his great strides soon arrived beside the boulder. So great was his annoyance that he lifted his sword and split the rock in two.

To this day, you can see this split rock, and it's said that anyone who walks through it three times – on the third occasion the boulder will close in on them. We don't know anybody who has tried so far!

11
The Dabharchú –
Hound of the Deep

It is said that lurking about the bed of Lough Ness in Scotland is a great monster and it seems that it is still there.

In the Yeats Country, on the edge of the boundary between Sligo and Leitrim, lies Glenade Lake. Could it be that another monster still lurks there?

Almost 300 years ago, and right up until recently in Ireland, women washed the clothes on the edges of lakes and rivers. The water was free-flowing, and there was the chance to catch up on local news from all the other 'washers'.

Two brothers named McLoughlin lived near the shore of the Glenade Lake, and one of them, Terence, had just taken a wife named Grace Connolly. As a young bride, Grace went to the edge of the lake to wash the clothes for her household. She was new to the area and so was alone as she washed. She hummed a tune to herself to have a good rhythm for the washing.

As she hummed, she thought that she was splashing quite a lot. She stopped washing for a moment, and still the splashing continued. She looked out from the

shore of the lake and could hardly believe her eyes! She rubbed her eyes – was she dreaming?

She let go of the clothes and shrieked in terror as the monster made its way in her direction. What rose before her was half-hound, half-serpent. Its ugly form came straight for her. She turned to run, but. . . it was too late. Grace knew nothing of the Dabharchú – the Hound of the Deep in Glenade Lake. She screamed for help but before her back was fully turned to the lake, the Dabharchú had claimed her life – the monster attacked her, she was knocked unconscious and Dabharchú and Grace disappeared from sight. Terence McLoughlin thought that he heard screams, in a voice which resembled Grace's, coming from the direction of the lake.

He knew the legend of the Dabharchú and as if by instinct he grabbed his gun. He ran towards the lake and saw the clothes floating on the water, but no sign of Grace, his bride!

Suddenly he heard a splash, and the Dabharchú once again stretched its ugly neck and head out from beneath the surface of the lough. Terence McLoughlin took aim and shot the Dabharchú dead. But as the monster's serpentine body dropped, an unnatural yell was heard from the lake and the sound travelled for miles around. McLoughlin was distraught having seen the vicious Dabharchú and having suffered the loss of Grace, his wife.

The wild shriek-like roar which had emanated from the lake drew the neighbours from far and near. One old man said: 'Terence, according to the old story, there are two Dabharchús, one is companion to the other. The strange shriek which you heard was the Dabharchú's companion mourning the loss of its loved one. And now, according to the legend, either you or the Dabharchú must die. My advice to you would be to get away as far as you possibly can from the Glenade lake, and do not ever return for fear of the Dabharchú.'

Terence's brother was beside the lake attempting to comfort his brother. He heard the words of the old man and said: 'Brother, we cannot risk the second strike of the Dabharchú. I'll go with you. We'll saddle our horses and ride fast over Ben Bulben.'

Neighbours helped, and very soon the McLoughlins rode off. In hot pursuit came the Dabharchú. Although you might imagine that the combination of serpent and hound living in a watery home would not produce great speed for travelling on earth, this was not so. With strange, slithery, athletic movements the Dabharchú pursued the McLoughlins. The anger caused by the killing of the companion spurred on the monster. The Dabharchú followed secret paths and waterways. The McLoughlins followed the old roads.

By now, they were on flat land again, on the far side of Ben Bulben and on high ground overlooking the ocean. They had arrived at Cashelgarran where there was an old O'Connor castle as well as an old fort. Horses and men were exhausted and they sheltered for a rest in the walls of the castle.

The Dabharchú was hot on the trail. Having sailed down the mountain on the Grange river, it approached Cashelgarran from the opposite side to

the horses. With a vicious lunge forward, the Dabharchú killed the first horse within the walls. But Terence
McLoughlin quickly pulled out his sharp, long dagger
and the Dabharchú was impaled on the dagger with
no escape route, as these were blocked off by one
dead and one live horse.

And now, no monster lurks in the lake at
Glenade. . . unless there is a third Dabharchú.

12
The Mistaken Laws
of Honour

Folktales 'happen'. Some are very old and some are not so old. Being about two hundred years old this story of 'The Laws of Honour' is not so old, but yet it has passed into the folk memory.

In the eighteenth century, fire-eating was in great repute, and when asking about a young person's qualifications the question, 'did he ever blaze' would usually be asked. And then, as well as blazing, duelling was in vogue in those times. Sligo had many schools for duelling in the nineteenth century and rules were strict, and governed by special codes and points of honour.

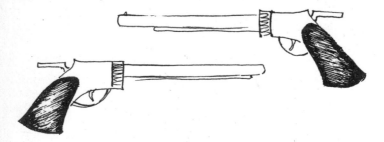

It happened that a priest named Father Burke was watching the sea-shore at Tireragh one stormy evening when he spotted a ship in distress. He felt helpless but dashed to the house of the nearest military man in the area – a Major Hillas. The Major acted swiftly and effectively. He boarded the boat. The Captain had already drowned. The ship foundered. But Hillas managed to save the crew and to save the vessel as well. Before the job was completed the ship was boarded by another Sligoman – this time it was John Fenton who had spotted the ill-fated vessel from the shore. Hillas' hour of glory was over. Sharp words rose between the two men. Fenton threatened to throw Hillas, the rescuer, into the sea and followed this up later with a challenge to Hillas.

A few days later Fenton's cousin, Thomas Fenton, took charge of the wreck, and boarded with the Castletown yeomen. Hillas became very annoyed, and so the scene was set for the challenge to be pursued and for the duel to take place.

The grave of Queen Maeve lies in splendour on the top of Knocknarea and in its shadow at Kilmacowen the scene for the duel was set. The duel was to be between Major Hillas and Thomas Fenton. Each duelist was entitled to a 'second'.

Fenton used his cousin John. Hillas had as his 'second' a Captain Ferrall, a noted duelist and as Ferrall was lame and in his late seventies, the 'second' position was passed to a Loftus Jones, and a Jack Taaffe 'assisted' also!

The rules of duelling are strict. In Sligo, pistols were used, though in Galway and elsewhere swords were preferred. Tension was high in the early morning – on the one side the two Fentons and on the other Hillas, and the three 'seconds'. Many versions of what happened in the moments which followed were proposed. Some say that with great adroitness Fenton placed his cousin on the ground, put the pistol in his hand and 'squared' him. Some say he stood too long having final words with him and that this allowed Thomas to look over his shoulder and take deliberate aim at Hillas.

On the other side, the various 'seconds' seemed to create disarray. Hillas said: 'I'm sorry that the mistaken laws of honour oblige me to come here and defend myself and I declare to God I have no animosity to any man or woman on the face of the earth.'

With that, Hillas threw off his coat to reveal tight black sleeves attached to his waistcoat – usually, billowing white sleeves made easier positioning targets.

Fenton was first to fire. Hillas' shot was quick to follow but too late in the event. He dropped dead on the first shot.

Court proceedings followed the sad end of Major Hillas who had so bravely saved so many lives. The court was crowded, the proceedings were long, and the jury was absent for a very short time. The Judge had declared that: 'Hillas had perhaps entangled himself on the subject more than he ought.'

The Fentons were acquitted and there ends the story of a famous Sligo duel.

13
King of
the Birds

The wren, though tiny, is said to be the King of the Birds. To this year, on St Stephen's Day, 26 December, the Wren Boys or Wran Boys or Mummers disguise themselves and travel from house to house entertaining the people. The custom is firm in the north of the Yeats Country.

The wren is not a very contented bird, unfortunately, and brings news of a death to some families. It has been said that since Christianity the wren is not highly regarded – the robin was trying to pull the thorns out of the crown of thorns while the wren was driving them inwards.

The wren in our story borrowed money from another bird. However, when the other bird demanded repayment, the wren refused. So the other bird called in the law, and called on the police to serve a summons. The policebird arrived at the wren's nest, and looked at all the little wrens chirping away, but there was a problem – the police could not distinguish mother from daughters.

The policebird knew how vain mother wren was and so began to praise her, although the policebird

kept looking from one to the other to check on the reaction. Mother wren began to preen her feathers with all the praise she heard from policebird. Quickly, policebird served the summons.

Mother wren was enraged and incensed. How dare they serve a summons on her! She immediately sought revenge. The wren visited the summons-server's husband and kissed him. The policebird was filled with rage and jealousy.

And so the poor little wren maddened yet another bird! And each St Stephen's day, the torture comes from humankind.

14

Diarmuid
Agus Gráinne

A pity beyond all telling
Is hid in the heart of love;
The folk who are buying and selling,
The clouds on their journey above,
The cold wet winds ever blowing,
And the shadowy hazel grove
Where mouse-grey waters are flowing,
Threaten the head that I love.

W. B. Yeats

Ben Bulben is a strange and majestic mountain. Its top is flat, beautiful Alpine flowers grow on its side now, but long ago it is said that every night its 'door' opened and the Sidhe, the fairy people flew through the world. It was the favourite hunting place for Finn Mac Cumhail and his mighty army of warriors. One of the Fianna was Diarmuid, and the famous love story and flight of Diarmuid and Gráinne ended on the slopes of Ben Bulben.

Gráinne was a princess and daughter of the High King of Ireland, Cormac Mac Art. Her home was the great palace at Tara.

Diarmuid was one of the best liked and bravest of all Finn's army. He was named 'Diarmuid na mBan', or Diarmuid – the Lady's Man. Women were automatically attracted to him – he looked so handsome and his manner was kindly. As well as his bravery and good looks he had another special attraction. He had a 'ball seirce' which is a type of beauty-spot. This was hidden most of the time, but should any woman see it, then she fell under his spell, and could not help but fall in love with Diarmuid.

Finn Mac Cumhail was the leader of the Fianna. It was a strict and powerful army. To be accepted, a man had to be a poet knowing twelve books of poetry. He had to prove his athletic ability by running barefoot through the woods at top speed; without disturbing a rib of his plaited hair and without cracking a dry stick under his feet. Without slackening his pace he had to be able to take a thorn from his foot with his nail. At the time of our story, Finn still led the army, but by now he was growing old. His own son Oisín was in the Fianna, as was Oscar, the son of Oisín, who had been to Tir na nÓg.

Finn looked around for another wife and asked Cormac Mac Art, the High King, to permit him to wed his daughter, the Princess Gráinne. Cormac was a wise king. He was well known for his good judgement. The army of the Fianna was very important to the King. And so, the young Princess Gráinne was engaged to Finn, the ageing leader of the great Fianna.

From her earliest youth, Gráinne had listened to her father, as the King spoke words of wisdom. He told his children: 'When I was young, I listened in the woods, I gazed at the stars, I didn't put my nose into anybody's secrets, I was mild in the palace, I was not given to making promises, I had respect for the older people, I never said a bad word of anyone who was not there, and I was fonder of giving than taking.'

At the same time, he told his children that they must not be lazy, or bad-tempered, or sleepy, or mean with their friends or envious of others. He told them never to curse or to be moody at a party and finally, never to break an appointment.

Gráinne had been schooled by her father the King, and now she was about to be married to Finn. A great feast was held to celebrate the engagement. The feast was held in Tara which Cormac the King had rebuilt. It was beautiful and spacious with pillars of cedar ornamented with plates of bronze. The walls were white, with patterns of red and blue. All the Fianna were invited to the feast, as well as all the Kings and Queens of Ireland.

Gráinne saw Diarmuid Ó Duibhne among the Fianna. She fell in love with Diarmuid and began to plan an escape for herself from the marriage with Finn for which she had no heart. She whispered to Diarmuid of her love and, although he was attracted by Gráinne, he was reluctant to elope with her as he knew what the consequences would be. When Gráinne recognised how impossible it would be for Diarmuid to steal a wife from Finn, the leader of the Fianna, she saw that only one course was open to her. She put Diarmuid 'under geasa' to elope with her. Now a geasa is a very solemn pledge which cannot be broken. The die was cast. Gráinne's plan went into

75

action. She poured drinks for all at the feast except for Diarmuid and his truly faithful friends. They were four, Oisín (the son of Finn), Oscar, Caoilte and Mac Lugh. A great drowsiness fell over all in Tara's halls. Soon they were asleep and Diarmuid and Gráinne with the help of the four friends set out on a flight which was to last seven long years.

Diarmuid and Gráinne fled westwards from Tara. A chariot took them to the banks of the river Shannon. Diarmuid carried Gráinne across the great river. There Diarmuid built a small hut. That was the first 'leaba' or bed of Diarmuid and Gráinne. This was to be the first of many beds and resting places because when Finn awoke in the great hall of Tara, and found that Gráinne and Diarmuid were missing his anger was unimaginable. His pride was deeply hurt, he felt that the trust which he had placed in Diarmuid had been dishonoured, and his jealousy that he now had Gráinne his beautiful princess for a wife knew no bounds. He summoned the Fianna's tracking men, the Clann Navin, and in his rage he ordered them to capture Diarmuid and Gráinne, and to take them both back so that they could face their punishment.

The Clann Navin lost the tracks at the edge of the Shannon ford, and Finn roared that unless they took up the track again speedily, all of them would be hanged on the edge of the ford.

Although Diarmuid had a good hiding place surrounded with a barricade of seven doors facing seven different parts of the wood, the Clann Navin tracked down the lovers, and a sentry of the Fianna was placed on every side. Although Diarmuid could have

76

escaped through the doors guarded by his four faithful friends, he would not do this, as he knew that Finn would take vengeance on them afterwards. He wanted to escape through the door which Finn himself guarded. Gráinne feared for his life. Escape seemed impossible. Now, Diarmuid had a foster-father called Aongus na Brugh. Aongus had many magical powers which he had learned from the wisest of the Druids. Aongus always protected Diarmuid and sensing the danger at the edge of the Shannon he flew to the aid of his foster-son. He spirited Gráinne from out of the hiding place under his mantle. Diarmuid refused to go under Aongus' mantle. He found one unguarded door, and with the help of two spears he bounded off to freedom to rejoin Gráinne who anxiously awaited him with Aongus.

Before Aongus parted from the lovers, who were overjoyed to be together again, he gave them these instructions:

> 'Do not go into any tree with only one trunk;
> do not go into any cave with only one opening;
> never land on an island with only one channel
> leading to it; where you cook your food, do not
> stay to eat it; where you eat do not sleep; and
> where you sleep tonight do not sleep tomorrow
> night.'

Diarmuid and Gráinne promised Aongus that they would do as he advised.

And so life was for seven years for Diarmuid and Gráinne. Diarmuid's faithful friends Oisín, Oscar, Caoilte and Mac Lugh sent messages ahead to their

77

hiding places, and so they fled before the Fianna and the Clann Navin. However, Finn's anger and jealousy did not seem to diminish.

Gráinne and Diarmuid began to become accustomed to their life of fleeing. They lived in close touch with nature. They were happy together. Diarmuid was a good hunter. It was a very different life for Gráinne who had grown up in the palace of her father the High King in Tara. Yet the good lessons which he gave her stood her in good stead.

And every night, as they lay down to sleep the people of the Faery sung this song over their bed;

We who are old, old and gay,
O so old!
Thousands of years, thousands of years,
If all were told:

Give to these children, new from the world,
Silence and love;
And the long dew-dropping hours of the night,
And the stars above:

Give to these children, new from the world,
Rest far from men.
Is anything better, anything better?
Tell us it then:

Us who are old, old and gay,
O so old!
Thousands of years, thousands of years,
If all were told.

During those seven years, flight became more difficult as time went by, because by now Diarmuid and Gráinne had to take their children along. First, they had a son called Donnachadh, then a son called Eochaidh and two more sons called Connla and Seal-bhach Searceach and one daughter whom they called Druineach Dhil. But Diarmuid's foster-father, Aongus was anxious that peace should be made between Diarmuid and Finn so that they could settle down and get away from a life of constant flight.

Aongus na Brugh encouraged Diarmuid to seek peace. Diarmuid outlined his conditions of peace and Aongus acted as intermediary between Diarmuid and Finn and with Cormac Mac Art, Gráinne's father. Although Finn's anger had not abated, he had grown tired of the chase and so peace was made. Finn indicated that he forgave Diarmuid and Gráinne for the wrong which he had suffered.

And so the lovers and their family settled down to a happy life in a place called Rath Ghráinne in the County of Sligo. Here the countryside was beautiful, the territory was good for hunting and they were a good distance from Tara – and trouble.

Diarmuid was happy to have made peace with Finn and it seemed as if life could begin anew for him. But one night in the middle of sleep Diarmuid was awakened by the distant sound of dogs barking. He decided he should investigate but Gráinne persuaded him to return to bed. Once again the dogs barked and Diarmuid became more agitated as though he were compelled to follow the sound. Once again, Gráinne induced him to remain. But the dogs barked loudly a third time, and Diarmuid was ensnared by the sound.

Gráinne attempted to dissuade him from investigating the barking, but he was determined to go. Gráinne sensed great danger, and said: 'Diarmuid if you must go, I strongly advise you to take with you your most powerful weapons – take with you the Moraltach (this was the sword of Mananann Mac Lir, the God of the Sea) and the Ga Dearg Dhoinn' (this red bow and arrow was the most deadly which Diarmuid possessed). But Diarmuid on this occasion did not seem to notice Gráinne's unease or advice, and said: 'No, I'll take only the Beagaltach and Ga Buí and Lamhouigh.' With a heavy heart, Gráinne watched Diarmuid leave Rath Ghráinne as he strode off with Mac an Cuil his hound on a chain by his side.

Diarmuid followed the direction of the dogs' barking, and it led him to Ben Bulben. As soon as the mountain loomed up before him, Diarmuid saw Finn and heard the sound of the Fianna hunting. It reminded Diarmuid of his days hunting with the Fianna.

Finn greeted Diarmuid and told him that the wild boar of Ben Bulben had killed fifty of his men that morning. 'I'll take a hand at hunting this boar,' said Diarmuid. It was then that Finn told Diarmuid a story he had never heard before. 'You must not hunt the boar, Diarmuid. You are "under geasa" never to hunt a boar – and especially not the wild boar of Ben Bulben.'

Long ago when Diarmuid was a boy his father had been asked to take a boy of Diarmuid's age as a foster-son. But Diarmuid's father had refused. It seems at the same time the young boy ran between Diarmuid's father's legs and somehow was killed as a result. Although an accident, Diarmuid's father was not forgiven by the boy's father Roc Mac Diochmhairc. He took the magic wand of Aongus na Brugh and gently placed it on the dead boy's head. The body changed, and a wild boar without ears and without tail ran out of the house. His father Roc then called out: 'I put you "under geasa" to live only as long as Diarmuid Ó Duibhne lives.'

'In order to save you Diarmuid,' said Finn, 'Aongus placed you "under geasa" never to hunt a boar. I have always kept you away from the boar hunt.' Diarmuid became suspicious of Finn then, and of the mysterious way in which the dogs' barking had lured him to Ben Bulben.

'Give me Bran,' said Diarmuid 'your favourite hound and I'll hunt the boar.' Finn refused to part with Bran his hound. It is said that Finn only cried twice in his life, and once was when Bran died.

As they spoke, the wild boar of Ben Bulben appeared at the peak. At that moment, Diarmuid thought of how foolish he was not to have taken Gráinne's advice. 'It is wrong for any man who does not take the advice of a good woman – she told me to take the Moraltach and the Red Arrow.'

He quickly drew the sword he carried, it hit the wild boar on its back. It didn't pierce a rib and yet it broke in two. Diarmuid was knocked off balance, he vaulted up from the ground in his usual fashion and landed on the boar's back. His head was facing the place where the boar's tail should be. The boar tore down the side of the mountain, trying to shake Diarmuid off his back. But Diarmuid's grip was firm. The boar tore off in a wild frenzy to the bottom of the mountain, and still Diarmuid was astride backwards. The boar dashed onwards until it came to the waterfall at Assaroe at the gateway to Donegal. The boar jumped the waterfall, back and forward three times, and still Diarmuid was astride.

The boar leaped again towards his 'home' on Ben Bulben. He pushed forward until once again he was on the top of Ben Bulben. Just as he turned from the peak of the mountain, Diarmuid grabbed another sword and dealt the boar a blow through his skull. Before he keeled over and died, he thrust his tusk into Diarmuid's side, and the hero's exhausted blood flowed freely from the wound.

As Diarmuid lay dying of the wound, Finn returned. He looked at Diarmuid now lying desolate and thought of how often he had looked splendid and had attracted the love of women a few years earlier. But although Finn pretended that he forgave Diarmuid when he made peace with him, his heart was still bitter, and jealousy had choked him.

'You have the power to save my life now Finn,' said Diarmuid.

'How?' Finn asked.

'You know full well,' said Diarmuid, 'that you only need to carry the pure water of a spring well in your hands and if I drink it my wound will heal.'

'There is no well on this mountain,' said Finn, knowing he lied.

By now, a number of the Fianna, and among them Diarmuid's true friends, had gathered round. 'There's a well just nine paces behind you, Finn,' said one of the Fianna. Finn reluctantly headed for the well, and placed his palms together so that the water was like a well inside. He began to walk towards Diarmuid – having decided that he would give him the healing drink. As he got close to Diarmuid he thought of the humiliation he had suffered because of Gráinne's running off with Diarmuid. He had been the laughing-stock of the Fianna, and so, he allowed the water to slip through his fingers.

Diarmuid reminded Finn of the many services which he did for him over the years as a loyal member of the Fianna. But Finn reminded Diarmuid that he took Gráinne, his bride, away from him. All the time Diarmuid was becoming weaker. Blood was flowing from his side and he mustered all his powers of persuasion so that for a second time Finn gave in and headed for the well.

He took the water between his palms again, and this time the Fianna held their breath as he approached the dying Diarmuid. All eyes were on Finn (who could think only of Gráinne) as he pretended to stumble over a small stone, and once again the precious water which could save the life of Diarmuid spilt out on the grass.

This time, Oisín, Finn's own son, and Diarmuid's true friend, threatened Finn. He castigated Finn the leader. He told Finn that there was a true bond between Diarmuid and himself, and he threatened Finn with a fight to the death if he would not save the life of Diarmuid. 'The rest of us are helpless,' finished Oisín. 'You alone can save his life.'

The light began to go from Diarmuid's eye as Finn returned to the well for the third time. This time, he filled his great palms full of water and approached the dying Diarmuid. He carried the water, and Oisín stared fixedly at his father's palms, and just as he approached Diarmuid and was about to give him the curing drink, Diarmuid's spirit left him and he breathed his last breath on the side of Ben Bulben.

His four true friends Oscar, Oisín, Caoilte and Mac Lugh took off their cloaks and placed all four of them on top of the body of Diarmuid of the Love Spot.

Gráinne, who was pregnant, stood outside Rath Ghráinne anxiously awaiting the return of Diarmuid. Over in the distance, she saw Finn approach with Diarmuid's hound Mac an Cuil by his side.

She knew the worst. Diarmuid's dog and Finn leading it. . . she fell to the ground, she sobbed and wept and lost the baby she was carrying. It is even said that she had been expecting triplets and all three were lost.

Gráinne sent 300 of her family to Ben Bulben to return with the body of Diarmuid. Aongus na Brugh sent 300 of his family to Ben Bulben and peace was made between them. Diarmuid's body was laid to rest at Brugh na Boinne.

Gráinne mourned for her dead husband and the father of her children. The children mourned. She gathered together hundreds of the clan of Diarmuid, and made them welcome at her house with a great feast. After the feasting, she addressed them all in a loud voice. She reminded them that the father of their clan was killed by Finn during a period of peace between them. Her last words to them were: 'Make your watchful attack.'

Aongus na Brugh mourned Diarmuid. He placed an aery spirit into him so that he could contact him sometimes.

And there ends the story of Diarmuid and Gráinne, the most famous lovers of olden times whose 'leaba' or beds can be seen to this day all over Ireland, and on the side of Ben Bulben there is a special resting place, called 'The Cave of Diarmuid and Gráinne'.

15

The Magician
Vera

A long time ago, there lived a magician or some
would say a witch called Vera. Her house or cave is
on the edge of the Mountain of the Two Birds. Vera
lived to a ripe old age, and sometimes in song and in
story she is called 'An Cailleach Bheara'!

While she lived, she possessed a cow, and as long
as she had it she enjoyed wealth and prosperity.
Sometimes neighbours in poor circumstances, knowing of the value of the cow, looked covetously at the
animal. They thought it would be so useful!

But the wise ones knew Vera's powers – and she
was older than the oldest person around and much
wiser! However, one man decided that now that she
was so old, he and his son would steal the cow from
Vera. At the dead of night they drove off the magical
cow. But Vera was no ordinary witch!

She heard the thieves as they passed before her cave.
Overcome with passion she quickly grabbed her oak
magic wand. As she touched the father and the son
they were immediately turned to stone. Unfortunately, so great was her frenzy that she slipped in the
darkness and the wand touched the cow and the cow

too was turned to stone. Vera had no way of bringing the cow to life again as the touch had been accidental.

And now the Cailleach Bheara, or Vera, was without her magical cow. She had lived for many hundreds of years, and now said:

> I am the Hag of Beare,
> Fine petticoats I used to wear,
> Today, gaunt with poverty,
> I hunt for rags to cover me!

She thought that the time had come to drown her 'fairy-life'. But for this she needed very deep water. She knew that she would not have far to travel to find a stretch of water deep enough to drown a 'fairy-life'. At the top of the Mountain of Two Birds is a lake. It is called the lake of the Two Geese. The old crone Vera considered her position:

> And my right eye has been taken away
> As down-payment on heaven's estate;
> Likewise the ray in the left
> That I may grope to heaven's gate.

So Vera travelled on the wings of the fairy wind to the top of the Mountain of Two Birds. The lake of the Two Geese * invited her in and to this day, she is there many, many leagues below. Listen!

---

* The local people say that there is an outlet from the bottom of the Lake of the Two Geese. We're not sure if it's true, but one man told a Punch journalist in the early 1900s that his brother dived into it for a swim. He was given up for lost until a few weeks later he received a cable from Australia to send him on his clothes!

16

The Enchanted Bridegrooms

Long, long ago there lived a wealthy and a good man named Fintan the Great in the southern part of County Sligo. He had three daughters and he was anxious that all three would marry good and prosperous husbands. How happy he was when he heard that three such young men were available, but lived at a great distance from Sligo.

The prospective bridegrooms were well recommended, and so Fintan invited them to his home. The three daughters were named Aoife, Beibhinn and Cred, and the bridegrooms were named Ainle, Conan and Diarmuid. There was great feasting and merrymaking when the weddings were arranged. Fintan was generous with his daughters – to the eldest Aoife he gave a dowry of her weight in gold. To his second daughter Beibhinn, the dowry was of her weight in silver, and to the youngest Cred her dowry was of copper. All were satisfied and when the ceremonies and feasting were over they bade farewell to their father in Sligo, all promising to return within a year and a day.

When the year was almost up, Fintan ordered that

great preparations be made to welcome the daughters and their husbands back home. On the day appointed the servants were posted to look out for the young couples, but although they stayed on the watch until well after nightfall, nobody appeared. Day after day they mounted watch, but there was no sign of Fintan's three beautiful daughters.

After two weeks, the sad father could bear it no longer. He began to make enquiries on all sides. No information could be found, and so Fintan sent off his son Ladra to try to trace his sisters and their husbands. When Ladra was a short distance from home, a red-haired man met him. He did not introduce himself and yet he was unusually friendly to Ladra, who poured out his troubles to the red-headed man.

The red-headed man knew the story. The husbands had been enchanted – Ainle had been turned into a ram, Conan had been turned into a salmon and Diarmuid had been turned into an eagle. The brides were all equally saddened and amazed by the disappearance of their husbands at first, and then gradually they came to realise that the ram, the salmon and the eagle each possessed the soul of the vanished husband.

The red-haired man promised to help Ladra to break the spells so that the bridegrooms could be released. They racked their brains, but neither seemed to know anything of how spells worked or could be broken.

They decided that it might be best to seek the help of all the animals of the 'husband's' species – ram, salmon and eagle. Word spread quickly in the animal kingdom that help was needed.

A great meeting was held on a distant shore. The eagle with its sharp eye told Ladra and the red-haired man that the Giant of Fomor had nursed a spite against the three brothers. When they returned following the weddings, they were off guard, and so the giant visited each to perform the trickery and to change the men into ram, salmon and eagle. The salmon told the red-haired man that he had seen a mole under the giant's arm when he went fishing, and he knew that the giant was vulnerable on that spot. The ram had seen the giant's spitefulness in action before, and knew that if either Ladra or the red-haired man could apply an egg to the mole under his arm that his power would be weakened.

The plan was laid – the giant raised his arm to cast his line for the salmon – the red-haired man aimed the egg directly at the mole under the giant's arm, watched by a bevy of rams, salmon and eagles. The aim was good and quite inexplicably the giant fell dead.

The red-haired man led Ladra to the houses of his sisters to find that great celebrations had begun.

On the death of the giant, to each bride the bridegroom had been restored. The red-haired man had hidden his identity out of fear – he was the brother of the three enchanted brothers!

In the morning, all the happy couples set out for Sligo to bring the good news to Fintan the Great who watched all day every day for the return of his daughters.

17
The Last Day

If you go to a funeral in County Sligo, look at the grave as the coffin approaches – you may see the spade and the shovel which have dug the grave left in the shape of a cross on top of the open grave.

This custom has come down to us from St Patrick. The Saint had a servant lad called Domhnaill who was one day collecting wood to make a fire. He had collected a very big and heavy bundle and, being young and his muscles not yet having developed fully, he could not lift the bundle.

He tried and tried and somehow it seemed to get heavier each time he touched it. Suddenly, Domhnaill saw that a small man, one of the Faery People, was lifting the bundle for him. Domhnaill thanked the Little Man as he left the bundle down where he was planning to set the fire.

'You must do me a favour in return Domhnaill,' said the Faery Man.

'Tell me your bargain,' said Domhnaill.

'Tomorrow, when St Patrick is at the most important part of the service of the Mass, ask him what will become of the Little People on the Last Day of Judgement.'

The Saint raised an eyebrow, as he was surprised that Domhnaill asked the question in the middle of the church service. 'They will all be lost,' came the Saint's quick reply.

Domhnaill was upset because he realised that this reply would not meet with the approval of the fairies – the Forgetful People.

St Patrick afterwards asked why Domhnaill had asked the question. When he discovered that his servant must return to the Faery folk with the reply, he advised him to dig a grave both wide and deep for himself and to stay there for one whole day. At the top of the open grave, the crossed spade and shovel must be placed to ward off the evil spirits.

'If you don't do this,' said St Patrick, 'the little people will tear you limb from limb in their rage.'

When the Faery man asked Domhnaill the question the next day:

'What does the Saint say will happen to the Little People on the Last Day?'

'They will be lost,' Domhnaill answered.

With that, shrieks and screams of a million fairies were heard. A storm broke out, lightning flashed and thunder rolled. Domhnaill was safely buried beneath his cross in the ground. The fairies began in a fearful vengeful mood and their cries ended up as a plaintive wailing.

Domhnaill stayed underground for two whole days. Then it was safe to emerge. Ever since the crossed spade and shovel adorn the newly opened graves in these parts.

Bibliography

Sligo and its Surroundings, Tadgh Kilgannon, Kilgannon & Sons Ltd., 1932.

The Yeats Country, Sheelah Kirby, The Dolmen Press, 1962.

Place Names in the Writings of William Butler Yeats, James McGarry, Colin Smythe, Gerrards Cross, 1976.

Sligeach, Oifig an t-Solatháir, Baile Átha Cliath, 1944.

Early Irish Myths and Sagas, Jeffrey Gantz, Penguin Books, 1981.

A Celtic Miscellany, Kenneth Hurlstone Jackson, Penguin Books, 1971.

Fairy and Folk Tales of Ireland, Ed. by W. B. Yeats, Pan Books Ltd., 1979.

Lough Gill Cruise Commentary, Mary Sweeney.

Tóraícht Dhairmada Agus Ghráinne, Neassa Ní Shé, Longman Brún agus Ó Nualláin, 1971.

Les Druides, Françoise Le Roux, Presses Universitaires de France, 1961.

The Collected Plays of W. B. Yeats, Macmillan & Co. Ltd., 1963.

The Collected Poems of W. B. Yeats, Macmillan & Co. Ltd, 1933.

The Adventures of Finn Mac Cumhal, T. W. Rolleston, The Mercier Press, 1979.

The History of Sligo Town and County, Archdeacon O'Rorke, J. Duffy & Co. Ltd.

The Celtic Twilight, W. B. Yeats, Colin Smythe, Gerrards Cross, 1981.